Apr 2019

MALCOLM X

BY JOAN STOLTMAN

Please visit our website, www.garethstevens.com. For a free color catalog of all our high-quality books, call toll free 1-800-542-2595 or fax 1-877-542-2596.

Cataloging-in-Publication Data

Names: Stoltman, Joan.
Title: Malcolm X / Joan Stoltman.
Description: New York : Gareth Stevens Publishing, 2019. | Series: Heroes of black history | Includes glossary and index.
Identifiers: ISBN 9781538231319 (pbk.) | ISBN 9781538230190 (library bound) | ISBN 9781538233115 (6 pack)
Subjects: LCSH: X, Malcolm, 1925-1965–Juvenile literature. | Black Muslims–Biography–Juvenile literature. | African Americans–Biography–Juvenile literature.
Classification: LCC BP223.Z8 S76 2019 | DDC 320.54'6092 B–dc23

First Edition

Published in 2019 by
Gareth Stevens Publishing
111 East 14th Street, Suite 349
New York, NY 10003

Copyright © 2019 Gareth Stevens Publishing

Designer: Katelyn E. Reynolds
Editor: Joshua Turner

Photo credits: Cover, pp. 1 (Malcolm X), 9, 25 Bettmann/Getty Images; cover, pp. 1–32 (background image), 7 courtesy of the Library of Congress; p. 4 http://www.latinamericanstudies.org/african-americans/UNIA-1924.jpg/ MassiveEartha/Wikipedia.org; p. 5 (main) Robert Parent/The LIFE Images Collection/Getty Images; p. 5 (inset) Voice of America: Learning English/Taterian/Wikipedia.org; p. 11 Time Life Pictures/Timepix/The LIFE Images Collection/ Getty Images; p. 13 MPI/Getty Images; p. 14 Underwood Archives/Getty Images; p. 15 Robert L. Haggins/The LIFE Images Collection/Getty Images; p. 17 Burt Shavitz/Pix Inc./The LIFE Images Collection/Getty Images; p. 19 Three Lions/Hulton Archive/Getty Images; p. 21 Pictorial Parade/Getty Images; p. 23 Pictorial Parade/Archive Photos/Getty Images; p. 24 NY Daily News Archive via Getty Images; p. 26 Fred Mott/Getty Images; p. 27 Erik McGregor/Pacific Press/LightRocket via Getty Images; p. 29 JON LEVY/AFP/Getty Images.

Printed in the United States of America

CPSIA compliance information: Batch #CW19GS: For further information contact Gareth Stevens, New York, New York at 1-800-542-2595.

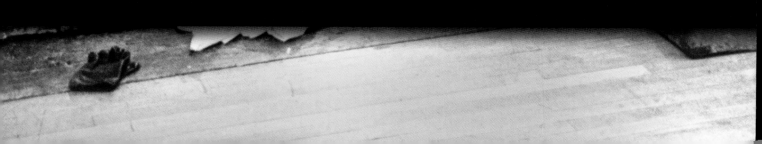

CONTENTS

Words in the glossary appear in **bold** type the first time they are used in the text.

BORN IN VIOLENT TIMES

Malcolm X was born as Malcolm Little on May 19, 1925, in Omaha, Nebraska. The **violence** that would follow him throughout his life began before he was even born.

A few weeks before Malcolm was born, members of the Ku Klux Klan (KKK), dressed in white robes and carrying guns, surrounded his house. They screamed for Malcolm's father, Reverend Earl Little, to come out and face them. This wasn't Reverend Little's first **death threat**. It wouldn't be his last. Malcolm's family was often in danger, partly because they were black, but also because Reverend Little was an active member of the UNIA.

WHAT WAS THE UNIA?

Started by Marcus Garvey in 1918, the UNIA (Universal Negro Improvement Association) is a large, influential black nationalist organization in the United States. Black nationalists believed that blacks should have their own country or state to live in separate from whites because peace was not possible while living together. Garvey wanted to start a new country in Africa.

UNIA parade

KKK

The KKK is a group that believes white Protestants are superior to all other groups of people. It was very well-known in the 1920s.

VIOLENCE IN HIS CHILDHOOD

For his family's safety, Reverend Little moved them first to Wisconsin, then to Indiana, and finally to Lansing, Michigan, in 1928. Soon after the Little family arrived, an angry white mob burned down their house. The police and firefighters refused to help. Malcolm was 4 years old at the time.

Despite this, Reverend Little didn't quit. He moved his family to a new home and continued his work. But, in 1931, Reverend Little died. It is unknown what happened to him and whether or not his death was an accident. After his father's death, Malcolm's family was left with little money.

NORTHERN RACISM

Sometimes people think of **racism** in history as being a Southern problem, but it was a serious, widespread issue in the North, too. Northern racism was different. It prevented black Americans from getting good jobs, housing, education, and more. Northern blacks were also subject to police violence.

6

Discrimination often pushed blacks out of white neighborhoods and into quickly built and poorly maintained parts of cities called ghettos.

7

Because she had no money, Malcolm's mother, Louise, made meals using dandelion greens from the street. Malcolm soon began stealing from food stores to feed his family. Louise became unwell after her husband's death. In 1939, she was moved to a hospital to be cared for. She would remain there for 26 years. The Little children were sent to foster homes. Despite all of this, Malcolm did well in school and was even class president! But in eighth grade, he told his teacher he wanted to practice law, and he was crushed when told that blacks could not go to law school. Malcolm soon gave up and dropped out of school at age 15.

JOB DISCRIMINATION

In the early 1900s, many black Americans from the South began moving to the North. Northern blacks worked in unskilled labor positions, like factory and service jobs. These jobs paid poorly and were sometimes even dangerous. Discrimination rules forbidding blacks at many colleges made it nearly impossible for blacks to learn enough to work skilled jobs and improve their economic situation.

By the 1920s and 1930s, large conflicts between blacks and whites, called race riots, were taking place across the country—even in the North—as discrimination and racism continued.

9

TURNING TO CRIME

In 1941, Malcolm moved to Boston, Massachusetts, to live with his half sister, Ella. He found a job shining shoes but soon turned to selling drugs and stealing. He was arrested three times in 5 years. His final arrest, when he was only 21 years old, earned him 10 years in prison.

HARLEM, 1935

The **Great Depression** was a tough time for many Americans, but black Americans may have suffered the worst. On March 19, 1935, about 10,000 blacks in Harlem rioted after hearing a fake story about a white policeman killing a black Puerto Rican teenager. They attacked white-owned stores and buildings because of this and anger over discrimination and living conditions.

While in prison, his brother Reginald visited from Detroit, Michigan. Reginald and Malcolm talked for hours about black societies, history, **culture**, and slavery. Reginald was a member of a new, black-only religion called the Nation of Islam (NOI), which was started in Detroit in the 1930s.

Malcolm went by the name "Detroit Red" while in the crime world of Boston and Harlem, a part of New York City.

TURNING AWAY FROM CRIME

Malcolm wanted to learn more about what the NOI believed, but he could not read well enough to understand history books. Eventually he was moved to a prison with a great library, guest speakers, and educational programs. After educating himself, he spent day and night reading history. Every week he practiced speaking in front of others, too.

Malcolm taught several other prisoners about the NOI. He then led them in a prisoner **protest** to see that their religion's rules—like not eating pork—were taken seriously. He left prison in 1952 after serving 6 years.

THE NOI

The Nation of Islam shared some ideas with the religion of Islam, but became a separate faith with its own views about history. At the time, its followers believed that whites were evil and blacks were superior to them. The NOI required that members not drink alcohol, do drugs, or smoke. They always had to have clean hair, nails, and clothes. Like the UNIA, members of the NOI were black nationalists.

When he joined the NOI, Malcolm changed his last name from "Little" to "X." This was a way of taking back power, since many African American family names came from masters during slavery.

13

A POWERFUL LEADER EMERGES

Within a year, Malcolm began training in Chicago, Illinois, under Elijah Muhammad, an NOI leader. Muhammad trusted Malcolm so much that he was soon sent to start temples in Boston, Massachusetts, and Philadelphia, Pennsylvania. By 1954, Malcolm was head of Harlem's temple, Mosque No. 7, the second largest NOI temple. He spent 10 years leading that temple, traveling often to spread the religion.

A GROWING RELIGION

Malcolm was determined to spread the religion that he felt had saved his life. He preached on the streets and started the NOI newspaper *Muhammad Speaks*. He also developed a prisoner and drug-user program to turn lives from crime toward the NOI. Largely due to Malcolm's efforts, the religion grew from 400 members in 1952 to 500,000 a decade later.

In 1959, a TV special—*Nation of Islam: The Hate That Hate Produced*—brought the religion, and Malcolm, national attention. From then on, Malcolm was often asked to speak, often in the national news. In 1963, he was named NOI national minister, the second highest position after Muhammad.

Malcolm X holds up an issue of *Muhammad Speaks.*

Malcolm met his wife, Betty, in 1958 after she joined the Harlem NOI temple that Malcolm led. They would go on to have six daughters, but the last two, who were twins, would never meet their father.

15

OPINIONS AND VIEWS

Malcolm's opinions often shocked people. He said Dr. Martin Luther King Jr. and other black **civil rights** leaders were fools for working with white people. He hated that they were trying to end segregation, or the forced separation of races. He thought the races should stay separate. He felt that racism made blacks hate themselves, and he pushed for black pride. He told blacks to **defend** themselves against violence, which was a very different message from the nonviolence preached by King.

White people feared that Malcolm's words would inspire violence against them. Black civil rights fighters thought that he ruined their progress by making blacks look angry and dangerous.

THE 1963 MARCH ON WASHINGTON

King gave his "I Have a Dream" speech at the March on Washington in 1963, which was one of the most famous civil rights events. Malcolm X said that the event did nothing to help blacks. Both leaders had the same goal of equal rights for blacks, but they never saw eye to eye on how to achieve them.

16

MALCOLM X SAID . . .

"I SEE AMERICA THROUGH THE EYES OF THE VICTIM. I DON'T SEE ANY AMERICAN DREAM; I SEE AN AMERICAN NIGHTMARE."

"A MAN IS EITHER A CITIZEN OR HE IS NOT A CITIZEN."

"BE NONVIOLENT ONLY WITH THOSE WHO ARE NONVIOLENT TO YOU."

"WE WANT FREEDOM BY ANY MEANS NECESSARY. WE WANT JUSTICE BY ANY MEANS NECESSARY. WE WANT EQUALITY BY ANY MEANS NECESSARY."

"I BELIEVE THAT IT IS A CRIME FOR ANYONE TO TEACH A PERSON WHO IS BEING BRUTALIZED [HARMED] TO CONTINUE TO ACCEPT THAT BRUTALITY WITHOUT DOING SOMETHING TO DEFEND HIMSELF."

Malcolm always proved to be a powerful speaker who could gather crowds and get people to think.

BREAKING AWAY

In 1962, police rushed into the NOI temple in Los Angeles, California, and killed a member. Malcolm was ordered not to protest the police violence. In 1963, he was banned from working with civil rights groups. To stop Malcolm from preaching about politics, Muhammad required ministers to submit speeches for approval. Malcolm began to have a problem with Muhammad's rules in the NOI.

When President John F. Kennedy was killed, Muhammad ordered NOI ministers to remain silent. But Malcolm spoke, saying that the violence was the consequence of a violent society.

VIOLENCE INCREASES

During the 1960s, America was dealing with increasing political violence. In 1963, a black church in Alabama was attacked, and four little girls were killed. Later that year, civil rights leader Medgar Evers was killed. There were over 150 mass violence episodes, called riots, during the 1960s. Most of these happened soon after the death of Martin Luther King Jr.

In 1957, NOI member Hinton Johnson was attacked and jailed by police in Harlem. Malcolm organized a protest outside the police station, shouting for Hinton to be taken to a hospital. This was one of the first times Malcolm X made national news.

19

MANY CHANGES IN 1964

After he was silenced, Malcolm left the NOI and started Muslim Mosque, Inc. (MMI). MMI organized action and welcomed blacks of any religion. Many people joined.

THE CIVIL RIGHTS ACT OF 1964

In 1964, Congress passed the Civil Rights Act, which banned discrimination in jobs and public places. Malcolm said, "After the bill was signed, three civil rights workers were murdered in cold blood. . . . Well, any time you live in a society supposedly [based upon law] and it doesn't **enforce** its own laws . . . then I say those people are **justified** to **resort** to any means necessary to bring about justice where the government can't give them justice."

Angry that Malcolm had started a competing group, members of the NOI spread lies about him. Malcolm responded by revealing how Muhammad had broken the NOI's rules. When the NOI newspaper said that "such a man as Malcolm is worthy of death," members began sending him death threats and trying to hurt him.

But Malcolm kept working. In 1964, he converted to a new faith, Sunni Islam, while in Saudi Arabia. Now friends with Muslims of many races, his thinking began to change.

Under his new Muslim name, el-Hajj Malik el-Shabazz, Malcolm traveled to the Middle East and Africa twice in 1964. After the first trip, his message changed from civil rights to human rights and expanded to include blacks from all over the world.

21

Malcolm returned to America and founded another group, the Organization of Afro-American Unity (OAAU), based on the new beliefs he formed while traveling. To spread awareness about the suffering of African Americans, he went back to Africa to speak to world leaders and their governing bodies on behalf of the OAAU.

Back in the United States, he preached about hope for a peaceful end to America's race problems. This was a new Malcolm. But the American press continued to push his old messages of self-defense and hatred of whites. Malcolm's continued attention in the American media angered members of the NOI. They tried to kill him at least four times and made many other death threats.

THE OAAU

Malcolm saw a direct connection between the **oppression** he saw of blacks in Africa and his experiences as an African American. He concluded that black people everywhere shared the struggle of being oppressed, and he formed the OAAU in response. By encouraging education, community building, organization, and voting, the OAAU worked to end oppression.

Even though Malcolm's mind-set had changed, the American media continued to present Malcolm as an angry man.

23

DEATH

Malcolm had almost figured out his next plan to help black Americans and blacks everywhere. There were a lot of new ideas and beliefs to sort through, but in the meantime, he moved forward with making speeches and protests against racism. He would never get the chance to go down a new path, though.

On February 14, 1965, his house was set on fire while he and his family slept inside. They all survived. A week later, while he was standing on stage at the Audubon Ballroom in Harlem, Malcolm was shot multiple times, in front of his wife, children, and a few hundred OAAU members.

WHO DID IT?

No one knows for sure who killed Malcolm X. Three NOI members went to prison for the murder. One of them, Talmage Hayer, was caught at the scene and admitted to having done it. Years later, in 1978, Hayer confessed that four other men, not the other two in prison, helped him plan and commit the murder.

24

DAILY NEWS
NEW YORK'S PICTURE NEWSPAPER ®
10¢
Vol. 46. No. 207   New York, N.Y. 10017, Monday, February 22, 1965   WEATHER: Partly cloudy, cold, windy.

MALCOLM X MURDERED

Gunned Down at Rally

Malcolm X, 39, is carried from Audubon Ballroom, 166th St. and Broadway, after he was shot while addressing a rally of his followers yesterday afternoon. He was declared dead at the Vanderbilt Clinic of Columbia-Presbyterian Medical Center within 15 minutes of the attack. Two men were taken by force from a howling mob of Malcolm's followers who were pummeling them on the street after the assassination. The slim Negro leader had been charging the Black Muslims with plotting to kill him ever since he defected from the group a year ago.

Story on page 3

People gathered to pay their last respects to Malcolm X at his funeral in Harlem, New York. He was 39 years old.

25

THE AUTOBIOGRAPHY

In the month before his death, Malcolm had finally finished telling author Alex Haley his life story. The two men met over 50 times in 2 years to talk through it all. *The Autobiography of Malcolm X, as Told to Alex Haley* sold 6 million copies worldwide from 1965 to 1977. It continues to sell copies today.

The book begins before Malcolm's birth and goes through his times as Malcolm Little, Detroit Red, Malcolm X, and el-Hajj Malik el-Shabazz. It inspired the Black Power movement of the 1960s and 1970s, and it has been especially popular with black youths over the years.

THE BLACK POWER MOVEMENT

The Black Power movement grew out of some African Americans' anger at the slow progress civil rights leaders were making. The movement pushed for social equality by celebrating black cultures and uncovering the lies in racism. Black Power followers often wore African-style clothing and hair to celebrate their culture.

Alex Haley

The truth was often exaggerated to create more excitement in the story of Malcolm's life, or autobiography. Still, his messages of black pride and community were seen as the central themes of the book. Most important, he pointed out that racism was the real problem, a message that still rings true today.

HIS LEGACY

In only 39 years, Malcolm proved that change and growth were possible. He changed his views throughout his life and wasn't afraid to admit he had changed his mind, which took great courage. He changed the country by bringing the deep history of racism in American society to light.

Malcolm told blacks to be proud, fearless, loud, and strong. He told them that they deserved respect and equality—that black lives mattered. He explained why African Americans had a right to be angry, by showing them how long and deep their history of discrimination and oppression was. Today, many still look to Malcolm X as a hero of black history.

MALCOLM X MATTERS TODAY

After the Civil Rights Act of 1964 and the Voting Rights Act of 1965, some people declared these victories the end of the fight. But these acts of Congress made only discriminatory laws illegal, not discrimination itself. Inequality and racism continue to oppress black people by affecting their education, living conditions, jobs, and treatment by police and court officials.

Malcolm's wife, Betty Shabazz, kept fighting for civil rights for the rest of her life. The ballroom where he was assassinated was turned into the Malcolm X and Dr. Betty Shabazz Memorial and Educational Center.

29

GLOSSARY

civil rights: the personal freedoms granted to US citizens by law

culture: the beliefs and ways of life of a group of people

death threat: a statement that you will be killed if you do not do what someone wants you to do

defend: to keep something safe

discrimination: unfair and unequal treatment of people because of their race or beliefs

enforce: to make sure people obey the law

Great Depression: a period of economic troubles with widespread unemployment and poverty (1929–1939)

justifiy: to provide a good reason for actions

oppression: to be treated in a cruel or unfair way

protest: an event at which a group objects to an idea, an act, or a way of doing something

racism: the belief that people of different races have different qualities and abilities and that some are better than others

resort: to do something or use something because no other choices are possible

violence: the use of physical force to harm someone or to damage property

FOR MORE INFORMATION

BOOKS

Fay, Gail. *Malcolm X*. Chicago, IL: Heinemann Library, 2013.

Pinkney, Andrea Davis, and Brian Pinkney. *Hand in Hand: Ten Black Men Who Changed America*. New York, NY: Jump at the Sun Books, 2012.

Shabazz, Ilyasah, and A. G. Ford. *Malcolm Little: The Boy Who Grew Up to Become Malcolm X*. New York: Atheneum Books for Young Readers, 2013.

WEBSITES

African American World for Kids E-Cards
pbskids.org/aaworld/ecards.html
Click through the cards to read about different points in African American history.

Chronology of the Life and Activities of Malcolm X
www.brothermalcolm.net/mxtimeline.html
Read through this timeline of Malcolm X's life.

Malcolm X Speaks!
www.columbia.edu/cu/ccbh/mxp/mxspeaks.html
Listen to excerpts from Malcolm X's speeches here!

INDEX

Daily Book Scanning Log

Name: _____   Date: _____   # of Scanners: _____

BIN #	BOOKS COMPLETED	# OF PAGES	NOTES / EXCEPTIONS
Bin 1			
Bin 2			
Bin 3			
Bin 4			
Bin 5			
Bin 6			
Bin 7			
Bin 8			
Bin 9			
Bin 10			
Bin 11			
Bin 12			
Bin 13			
Bin 14			
Bin 15			
Bin 16			
Bin 17			
Bin 18			
Bin 19			
Bin 20			
Bin 21			
Bin 22			
Bin 23			
Bin 24			
Bin 25			
Bin 26			
Bin 27			
Bin 28			
Bin 29			
Bin 30			
Bin 31			
Bin 32			
Bin 33			
Bin 34			
Bin 35			
Bin 36			
Bin 37			
Bin 38			
Bin 39			
Bin 40			

(BOOKS / LIBROS) TOTAL: _____ / 600

(PAGES/PAGINAS) TOTAL: _____

SHIFT: _____   STATION #: _____